Check out these Mystery/Suspense novels
by Giacomo Giammatteo.

Friendship & Honor Series:
Murder Takes Time
Murder Has Consequences

Blood Flows South Series:
A Bullet For Carlos
Finding Family (a novella, June, 2013)

Redemption Series:
Old Wounds (August, 2013)

No Mistakes Resumes

Don't Get Caught in the Moat

Giacomo Giammatteo

Inferno Publishing

Inferno Publishing Company
Houston, TX

For more information about this book visit: http://nomistakes.org

Edition ISBNs
Trade Paperback 978-1-940313-00-9
E-book 978-1-940313-01-6

Cover design by Maria Zannini of Book Cover Diva
Book design by Christopher Fisher

This edition was prepared for printing by The Editorial Department
7650 E. Broadway, #308, Tucson, Arizona 85710
www.editorialdepartment.com

Acknowledgments

The tough part of writing a book is not the writing, it's all the stuff that comes after that. I'll take credit for the writing. For the tough parts I am honor bound to thank the following:

My great copyeditor, Annette Lyon, from Precision Editing Group.

A fantastic graphic designer, Maria Zannini, for the book cover.

Christopher Fisher from The Editing Department, for the amazing layout and formatting.

And most importantly the army of beta readers who worked overtime to help me get this book into shape:

Rose, Aliza, Missy, Paul, Seeley James, John Maynard, Woody, Otto and Ries.

Special thanks to my grandsons, Joey and Dante. And *grazie mille* to my niece, Emiliana, who kept me company and shared coffee with me on many late nights.

Lastly, to my wife, Mikki, who puts up with all of my nonsense. Without her, these books wouldn't be worth writing.

Ti amo con tutto il mio cuore.

Note to readers:

I've seen resume books that were hundreds of pages long. I'm sure you have, too. You might wonder why this one is fewer than 100 pages. I'll tell you why—writing resumes is not that complicated. It *isn't* quantum physics.

You might also be wondering if this book can help you. There are no guarantees in life, but I'm confident that if you follow the advice in this book, you'll end up getting more interviews. You won't get all of them, but you should get more than you did before.

With that said, if you read this and feel there was something left out, or something you would have liked covered in more detail, email me and let me know. I read all my emails and I consider all suggestions when looking at updates.

No Mistakes Resumes

Don't Get Caught in the Moat

Contents

Introduction

I KNOW WHAT YOU'RE THINKING—why should I buy this book? What is it going to do for *me?*

This book has *one* purpose: to teach you how to write a great resume. A resume that won't get thrown in the trash, a resume that will help you get the *interview.*

This book challenges a lot of preconceived notions about resume writing. Many how-to books offer a variety of templates for writing resumes. Here we focus on *one* way: the *perfect* resume, the one gatekeepers won't dump in the trash.

I've been a headhunter for more than thirty years, which means that I've screened, scanned, skimmed, and perused[1] tens of thousands of resumes. I learned a lot during those years, but the one thing that has stuck with me most is the frustration of seeing the same mistakes over and over again. I understand how much people struggle with resume writing. If you're writing one, it goes without saying that this is a trying time in your life, and you're probably filled with anxiety. The last thing you need is mistakes in your resume. Unfortunately, this is when mistakes show up the most.

The frustration for me was knowing the problem is so easily fixed, so I decided to do something about it. This book is the result.

I'm going to be critical, but it's all geared toward helping you. So put on your thick skin. Arm yourself with a shield if you need to, but let's work through this together. We'll come out with the perfect resume.

This book is about language as much as it is about writing a resume; the two go hand in hand. Resumes and cover letters are where communication seems to fall apart. Sentences become bloated, words are misused, and ideas deteriorate. The lessons in this book will show you how to spot these problems and how to correct them.

What's the harm in a few extra words, you ask? When you are trying to pare (not *pear* or *pair*) your experience down to two pages that have *impact*, every word counts. More on that later.

Another thing you'll notice are side comments after certain words, as the example above with *pare* shows. These are words that I often see misused or questionably used on resumes and cover letters.

So if you're ready to construct the *perfect* resume, one that won't get thrown in the trash, let's move on.

No Mistakes Resumes:

Don't Get Caught in the Moat

WHY IS THIS BOOK SUBTITLED "Don't Get Caught in the Moat"? Writing a resume is hard, and while I was thinking of difficult things, storming castles came to mind. I imagined a medieval castle surrounded by a deep moat, with a gatekeeper wielding a sword and knocking job seekers off the drawbridge.

Play along with that concept, and I'll introduce you to the cast.

Gatekeeper—First guardian of the castle. Defender of the moat—also called Rose. She is the director of human resources for the castle. For those of you who may be wondering, I have a sister named Rose, who happens to be a director of HR. Other than that, they have nothing in common. (Except physical appearance, manner of speech, and they both say "jackass" a lot. A *whole* lot).

Me—Narrator. Headhunter supreme. Always opinionated. Never wrong.

You—the candidate for the job, aka the relentless one, slayer of dragons, savior of worlds, castle-storming knight-in-armor... and sometimes reduced to humble job seeker.

Wastebasket—How can a wastebasket be a character? In this story, anything can happen; in fact, the wastebasket is a primary character.

Now that you have been introduced to the main cast, let's get started.

Special note: At times you may think I come across a little sarcastic (or even a *lot* sarcastic) and that some of my examples and admonishments are harsh. I use this tone for one reason: to make a point. I want nothing more than for each and every one of you to have a perfect resume. Following the examples in this book will help you achieve that goal.

The Purpose of a Resume

NOW THAT WE'VE FINALLY STARTED, let's review what you already know.

- A resume *cannot* get you a job. Never! Won't happen.
- A resume has *one* purpose: to get you an interview.

I've seen people at the end of their rope, not understanding why they weren't called in for an interview when they know they fit the job perfectly. They're clueless that their resume, the one they thought was magnificent, is the culprit that kept them from getting the interview.

Have you ever wondered how certain movies become blockbusters, doing in excess of a billion dollars in sales, when your favorite show languishes and doesn't even earn enough to cover production costs? Or how a book becomes a bestseller when it seems like it was written by an imbecile? It's the same reason why the most qualified person doesn't always get the job offer. You have to know how to *sell* yourself.

You may be surprised at the process; most interviews don't happen because the resume is so compelling it convinces a gatekeeper that she *has* to see this person. Most interviews are the result of the "last man standing" principle. (*Not* principal) What's that, you ask? It's the process whereby the gatekeeper trashes intelligently screens out all the other resumes, and the few remaining ones get interviews.

In a perfect world, the gatekeepers search each resume for hidden talents and reasons why a person may fit the job, or how a person could help the company achieve its goals. But we don't have a perfect world, so when it comes to screening resumes, the process goes from "how can this person help us?" to "why *isn't* this person right for the job?"

I'm going to let you in on a little secret...

Resumes are boring

Every recruiter and every gatekeeper I know gets bored reading resumes. There is nothing new to say on a resume, and nothing you can do to impress the gatekeepers—except be what they're looking for. So don't try to be different for the sake of being different. Your resume should be your foundation—your rock. It needs to be *perfect*, not fancy.

Think of a house. The basis of good construction is a solid foundation—usually concrete—and then good, strong walls. Concrete isn't pretty. It doesn't come with bells and whistles or peripheral items. Concrete is there for one reason—to support your house. That's what your resume is like. It has one purpose also: to support your cover letter and get you an interview.

Kitchens and bathrooms sell houses

That may be true, but cracks in the foundation or walls send a potential buyer running. Think of your resume as the foundation—something rock solid with zero mistakes that focuses on accomplishments. Think of your cover letter as the kitchen and bathrooms—let it do the selling.

Back to the Gatekeeper

Right now, she's going through resumes with death rays coming from her eyes. At the first sign of something wrong, a resume can get trashed. Sometimes the resume just gets a red flag, but if it gets too many red flags, that resume is *gone.*

Your job is to write your resume *so perfectly* that the gatekeeper has no choice but to consider it. If you don't give them *any* reason to toss it, it *will* get reviewed. You'll need good experience to get through the castle gate. Don't let mistakes keep you out.

Let's Take a Look at an Imaginary Scenario

Assume you just got laid off after ten years with the same company. You're on your way home, punching the steering wheel, and hurting your hands. (Women are smarter than that, so if you're a woman you're driving home, you're gnashing your teeth and, perhaps, biting your nails.) But in this scenario you *are* a guy, so you are punching away and cursing the horrible drivers around you. The freeway seems full of them.

Getting home is taking forever. You feel like crap, and, to top it off, you don't even *want* to get home, because you'll have to tell your spouse what happened. How embarrassing is that? Your stomach roils, and you feel like throwing up; instead, you hit the dashboard and curse a few more drivers. Soon enough, *too soon*, you arrive home and put on the best face you can. When you walk in the door, your spouse looks at you with a curious expression.

"What are you doing home so early?"

You suck it up, swallow hard, and say, "I was fired."

"Fired? Why did they fire you? Your the best person they have in marketing."

You shrug. Your face flushes with embarrassment and shame. You do a masterful job of holding back tears until finally you muster the courage to look at your spouse.

"I was lead to believe they're cutting back in all departments. There's a lot of reasons, but the shrinking market for disk drives seems to be the big one."

Your spouse hugs you. You feel like crying—and hitting someone—but you sure welcome that hug. Now you'll have the energy to get to work and find that dream job.

Let's Put on the Brakes

Before we start on the dream job, let's take a look at that conversation. Did you find the mistakes in that bit of drivel? I hope so. If not, you have a *lot* more work to do than I thought. There were three. Look hard for them. Don't stop until you find them.

Okay, you can stop looking. If you noticed all three—bravo! (If you found more than three you're worse off than the ones who didn't notice them.)

I understand that seemed like trickery, but these three words needed attention. They are some of the most misused words in cover letters and resumes.

Let's Look at Them

The spouse said: "*Your* the best…"

It *should* be "*You're* the best…" (The contraction for *you are*)

You said: "I was *lead* to believe…"

It *should* be "I was *led* to believe…" (Past tense.) *This is the most common resume mistake.*

You said: "*There's* a lot of reasons…"

It *should* be "*There are* a lot of reasons" since *reasons* is plural.

I have to make a special comment about the last one. The word *there's* has crept its way into the top spot of grammar mistakes across all media. I see it misused in books, in articles, all over the internet, and constantly hear it on the radio, in movies, and on TV shows. Many people don't see a problem with a few mistakes. Trust me, gatekeepers *do*. And since the gatekeepers are the ones with control over whether or not you get in the door, you have to please them.

My Reaction to This

I have to tell you, I would have trashed a resume with those mistakes on it. Not because the person doesn't know grammar, but because the person who wrote the resume didn't put forth the effort to ensure it was done correctly. If I wanted to be a budding psychologist, I could infer that the person is possibly overconfident, lazy, has no eye for detail, doesn't care enough…the list goes on. And remember, a *lot* of gatekeepers are budding psychologists. Don't give them anything to analyze.

Now that we've been introduced (and you see what an ass I am) it's time to move on and learn how to write that perfect resume.

Mistakes

BEFORE YOU LEARN HOW TO write the perfect resume, you must learn that mistakes are your enemy. You only have about 10 seconds to get noticed—don't let a mistake get your resume trashed before you catch the gatekeeper's interest.

In your quest to get inside the castle, you won't have to actually fight a dragon or rescue a princess, and you won't (I hope) be dressed in a suit of armor, but you *will* have to battle human-resource and talent-acquisition screeners. A resume is the only weapon you're allowed, so it's imperative you do it right.

How to Do It Right

The mistake I see most often is the misuse of *lead* and *led*. I did a search of my database, which contains almost twelve thousand resumes. From the search results I pulled up all the resumes that used the word "lead." I randomly went through the first three hundred. In an astonishing 27%, the person had used the present tense *lead* instead of the past tense *led*.

Here is an example from a resume:

- Developed prototype for new product to revolutionize testing for…
- *Lead* efforts of twenty-seven engineers and brought in product on schedule and under budget.

As you can see, the first accomplishment was fine, done properly in the past tense using the word *developed*. The second, however, uses *lead* in the present tense, instead of *led*, which is the past tense of the verb.

This leads (present tense) me to believe that people don't have a good command of the English language. I was led (past tense) to this belief by seeing so *damn* many resumes with this same error.

This is one of the most common mistakes on resumes, but there are plenty of others. A few are listed below:

- Spelling errors
- Misuse of words
- Mixing up tenses
- Incorrect use of compound adjectives/modifiers
- Incorrect punctuation, including the dreaded semicolon.

Don't worry. We will get to them all in time. Have ~~patients~~ patience.

How to Construct
a Perfect Resume

OKAY, SO YOU LOST YOUR JOB. You took a few weeks to loaf, did all the chores you'd been putting off, and took a mini-vacation. You're ready to don your suit of armor and storm the castle gates. You investigated the castle and noticed it was being stormed by hundreds of people, all wielding resumes. So how do you get in when all of these people are ahead of you? And armed with resumes! Especially when the gatekeeper is guarding the entrance with scrutinizing eyes, ready to reject all but a few of the gazillions, or some such number, of resumes stacked outside the gate. (I don't know how many a *gazillion* is, but my mother used to say that *a lot* when she wanted to confuse us. Notice it is *not* one word, *alot* but *a lot.*)

To get in the gate, you must construct a resume that stands out from the masses. Let's look at the framework for building a great resume. Afterwards we'll go into detail on each section.

A Great Resume

Below is what many of the resumes I receive look like, as far as structure.

Name
Address
Phone number
Email address

Your name, address, phone number and email should be at the top, centered on the page. This is how it should be. Formatting will be discussed more later.

~~OBJECTIVE:~~ Absolutely not! *Do not* put in an objective. You'll notice I didn't waffle when I said that.

~~SUMMARY:~~ Not necessary. Yes, you heard me. *Not necessary.*

~~PERSONAL:~~ All the personal information you need to include should be at the top of the page. You *do not* need anything else.

SKILLS: This section is usually unnecessary. For some occupations it might be appropriate.

EDUCATION: *Always* include this, even if you don't have a degree. It's like ID at the airport. You *absolutely* have to have it or you *will not* get on the plane.

EXPERIENCE: The meat!

Companies worked for.

Titles of jobs held.

Dates of employment, and dates you held each position.

A brief description (a sentence or two) about each company. This is especially important if you aren't applying to a direct competitor. You can use this space to show that your experience is applicable. (More on this later.)

~~HOBBIES:~~ *Never* include.

CERTIFICATIONS AND LICENSES: Include if relevant.

PUBLICATIONS and PATENTS: I prefer to say "publications available upon request." If they are requested, that provides a chance for you to point out the relevant ones. For example:

"I noticed in the job description you want someone who has experience with X. I wrote several papers dealing with that subject and was granted a patent in that area."

This will have a lot more impact than just including them with the original resume. You can mention in a cover letter that you have patents/publications dealing with the areas of interest.

REFERENCES: It isn't necessary to include anything on the resume. A company presumes that you will provide references if discussions get to that point. If you feel that you *absolutely have* to put the word *references* on your resume, it's all right to say "references available upon request" or something to that effect. But don't *ever* list the actual references.

Now you have the basic sections of the resume, but before we get into specifics on each one, let's talk about formatting.

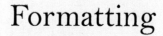

Formatting

Don't skip this section!

IT MIGHT BE THE MOST IMPORTANT section of all. This deals with the readability of your resume, and that affects the gate-keeper. Without the proper formatting, your resume is garbage—literally—because Rose will toss it in the trash.

I have never seen a resume tossed out because it was two or even three pages long, but I have personally tossed resumes where the person tried cramming too much into one page, reducing line spacing and font size until these tired old eyes could barely read it. I guess if I had increased magnification to 150% I could have, but guess what—I'm not going to bother. It's easier to toss it.

Okay, now let's look at formatting.

~~Alot~~ A lot of resumes start the same way, with your name, address, and contact information at the top of the page. I have seen it done differently, but I think most people prefer it centered on the page.

So instead of this:

Jane Doe
4543 Stressed Out Lane, San Francisco, CA 00000 * Home# (650) 555-5555 * Cell# (650) 555-5554 * janedoe@someserver.com

Do it like this:

Jane Doe

4543 Stressed Out Lane, San Francisco, CA 00000
Home# (650) 555-5555 * Cell# (650) 555-5554
janedoe@someserver.com

There are endless choices for font size, but I recommend that your name be in a 14-point bold font, and that the rest of the information be in 9-point. You can use 12-point for your name—even 16-point—but don't go bigger than that. You know those gatekeepers; they try to analyze you before ever meeting you. If you use anything higher than a 16-point font, they may think your ego is inflated. Anything less than 12, and they suspect low self-esteem. (So despite me saying there are endless choices, there really aren't. There are only a few—if you want the job.) My personal choice is Times New Roman, 12 point. It's not the prettiest font, but it's easy to read, universally accepted, and prints nicely.

Font:

Have you ever read a book where the fonts are too small...like this? **Don't do that!** The gatekeeper will toss that resume like an old ham sandwich.

And don't make them too large, either. It looks ridiculous!

Page margins:

Keep the margins so the document can be printed without adjusting them. One inch all the way around is fine. Some people prefer 1.25" on the left and right margin. Also, make certain that the header and footer have at least .5" so they don't adversely ~~effect~~ affect printing.

White space:

One of the worst things you can do is cram your resume onto a page. I know there's a lot of "advice" out there about keeping your resume to two pages. I have even heard some people say keep it to one page. You don't have to.

I can't stress enough the importance of making your resume easy to read. Don't try to cram your experience to fit a page count. No matter how many pages you need—*do not* go below single line spacing, and preferably not below a 12-point font.

A note is in order here. If you follow the rules in this book about which sections to include, and which to not, and if you don't get carried away with unnecessary responsibilities, your resume will probably be no longer than two pages.

The Easy Way

Plenty of "easy resume" templates are available on the internet. Some are free, and some you must pay for. What's common with most all of them is that they are "easy," and that is *precisely* the problem. I know you've heard the old saying that nothing comes easy. Resumes are no different. Doing a resume properly takes work. A lot of work. It is *not* easy. It may be one of the most difficult things you'll ever write.

Why are resumes so difficult? They're only two pages, right?

In reality they aren't. They are your life's work condensed to two pages. Two pages that must be *perfect*. Two pages that need to be checked and then checked again to ensure you have not missed anything.

- The formatting and fonts must be right.

- The presentation must be the best it can be.

- Your words must be crisp.

- Your accomplishments must have impact.

- And your work history must be precise.

Think of your resume as a reflection on you. Would you go to an interview with your hair unkempt? Teeth not brushed? Face dirty? Grime under your nails? Stinky?

Then don't send your resume out that way. Dress it up nice and pretty.

One final word on formatting—before you hit the "send" button, make sure that the "view" option is set at 100%. You want the person receiving your resume to view it in a normal state. If they want it bigger, or smaller, they can adjust it on their end.

Note: There is something to be said for sending your file as a PDF document instead of Word or another format. Anyone can open a PDF file, and the formatting doesn't get disturbed. I've seen Word and RTF files get trashed, but I have yet to see a PDF suffer. If you're dealing with a recruiter, you might want to send them a PDF *and* a Word file. If you're sending directly to the company you might opt for PDF—unless—they ask specifically for Word.

Skills

I'M NOT FOND OF A SKILLS SECTION, but I'll admit that in some cases it helps. A new college graduate, or someone who recently learned new skills but hasn't yet put them to use on the job, may want to include it. However, if you can show your skills in the accomplishments section, it's better. Example: Instead of putting in the skills section that you are proficient in C++, perhaps *show* it in the accomplishments section:

Designed new controller using C++...

Doing it this way *shows* that you not only have this skill, but that you have put it to practical use. If that's not an option, by all means put in a skills section and list your expertise. This could be especially helpful if the job description calls for expertise you have no other way of showing.

Computer skills, language skills, and other specialized areas fall neatly into a section like this. Of course they can always be brought to light in the cover letter, but having a skills section provides a good backup.

Other data that may require a separate listing are certifications, licenses, and patents. Professional memberships and associations are fine to list, but don't list personal things, like being on the board of your church, the PTA, or homeowners' association.

You could justify putting many other valid skills into a section like this. If it makes sense, do it. But ask yourself if it's *needed* to sell the resume, and if keeping it could in any way, shape, or form, get you screened out. If it still makes sense, put it in.

Point of View

POINT OF VIEW IS IMPORTANT in writing. I'm sure you've all read novels done in the first person point of view. This is okay in a novel. It is *not* okay in a resume. It makes you sound egotistical, as if you're bragging. It has the reverse effect of what you intended. Instead of impressing the one reading your resume, you alienate them.

School Reunion

Think of someone who tells you how good they are at something. Maybe you've seen someone like this at a school reunion. They're the ones talking about all they've accomplished and boasting of their successes. They are normally charismatic. You may even have fond memories of them. But soon you notice their sentences are riddled with "me, my, I, mine…" You tire of hearing about their new cars, the beach house, the vacations abroad. Your initial impression turns to one of disgust. Before long, you distance yourself from them.

Now think of the quiet person mingling with the crowd. The person who asks how *you* are, how the family is. The person who remembers nice things about *you* and how good *you* were in school. They remember your spouse's name, and, remarkably, even the names of your kids. They tell others gathered around how good you were at geometry. You bask in the limelight. After they leave, a different classmate tells you how successful that person has been—of their beach houses, private jet, the perfect family, the businesses they run. The impression is completely different, isn't it? You think highly of them. You're happy for them.

Point of View Differences

When you talk about yourself on the resume, you come across like the braggart. When you stick to the third person point of view—but without using pronouns like he or she—it gives the impression someone else is saying how good you are. The difference is dramatic.

The first person POV usually rears its ugly head in summaries, and it starts you off on the wrong foot. There are few worse offenders. I'm not saying a gatekeeper will trash your resume if it's done in first person, but she might put a red flag on it, wondering if you're a team player. As we've discussed before, you don't want red flags.

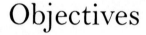

Objectives

Now that I know you won't make any grammatical errors—or at least that you won't misuse lead/led—let's focus on other mistakes you are bound to make.

What mistakes, you ask?

Let's see…how about like…putting an *objective* on the resume.

Some people advise against putting objectives on resumes. I go a little beyond that. I despise objectives. I would even go so far as to say I *loathe* them.

I did a quick search of my resume database and was not surprised to find that almost 30% of the people had objectives on their resumes.

Below are some (real) samples:

CAREER OBJECTIVE:

• Position that will utilize my education, background and experience, expand my knowledge and offer opportunities for personal and professional growth.

Take a close look at this. Did this person really think that objective would inspire a gatekeeper to fumble for the phone and invite him in for an interview?

Here's another one:

- Objective: A Senior Management position requiring innovative and creative approaches to the development and implementation of a solid business strategy based on a basic understanding of technology with a focus on the achievement of business and financial goals.

I read that three times. What the hell did he just say? I don't know exactly what he meant by all that, but if I were the gatekeeper, I wouldn't take the time to find out. You know where this is going, don't you? In the trash.

Okay, next one:

Career objective:

A Senior Director position where I will: Impact the business by delivering projects of strategic value. Establish a world-class Project Management culture, founded on state-of-the art best practice, integrated into Portfolio and Strategic Management. Make a long-term contribution with a positive impact and surpass all goals and objectives, and in short, improve the performance of the company.

I don't know about you, but I think this person certainly far surpassed my creative and boundless imagination in stating their objective. (I know—that's as confusing as the objective isn't it?) And by the way, did you notice all the words capitalized in these objectives? Words that *shouldn't* be. More on that later.

What were these people thinking? Did they really believe that a gatekeeper would let them into the castle with those lines as objectives? If they thought they would get across the moat with those objectives, they don't know ~~Rose~~, I mean the gatekeeper.

The Inside Scoop

For the sake of argument, and because I'm the one writing this book, let's assume that we'll rule out objectives as an integral part of the resume. We'll agree not to put objectives on resumes because they can't help you, and they *might* hurt. No matter what your objective says, unless it meets the vision this particular company has for the position, you have potentially screened yourself out.

A good objective—even a perfect objective—won't compensate for lack of experience, weak accomplishments, an unstable work history, or inappropriate education. A good objective *may* get you a nod of the gatekeeper's head, and keep her reading for a few more lines. But she'll do that *without* an objective too.

The Coffee Argument

Suppose Starbucks put a teaspoon of sugar into every cup of coffee. What do you think would happen?

- People who like less than a teaspoon of sugar would be unhappy.

- People who like more than a teaspoon would be unhappy.

- People who don't like sugar at all would be *very* unhappy.

In fact, the only people who would be happy are the ones who like *exactly* one teaspoon of sugar.

Putting an objective on a resume is just like that.

I have never seen or heard of the lack of an objective as being the reason for screening someone out.

Because this point is so important, I'll repeat it: **I have *never* seen or heard of the *lack* of an objective being the reason for screening someone out.**

Unless you can write me an objective that is *so* strong, *so* compelling, that it will make a gatekeeper want to bring you in for an interview right then without reading further, I suggest you leave it off your resume.

The Bottom Line

Leaving an objective off your resume will offend no one. No one will second guess you. No one will toss your resume into the trash can.

Dates

I LIKE TALKING ABOUT NOTHING more than dates. I don't mean the kind we had as teenagers or the kind you eat; I mean the dates on a resume. Why? Because this is where people seem to go hopelessly awry. The sad thing is that this is the easiest part of the resume to get right. All you have to do is learn where to put them—and, tell the truth.

Dates on a resume are like olive forks; there is no special slot for them in the silverware drawer. There *are* options: you could put them with the iced-tea spoons, or with the espresso spoons. You could even squeeze them in with the cocktail/shrimp forks, but regardless of where you put them, it always seems to be the wrong choice. That's because you have options. Having options confuses us, especially when it comes to resumes.

These are some of the questions I get asked about dates:

- Do I put them in the left margin?
- Do I put them on the same line as the company, but to the right?
- Do I right-justify the date?
- How about after each position if there are more than one in a company?
- Do I include the months or just the years?

- Do I spell out the months? Or use numbers?
- Do I include days?
- How do I handle gaps in employment?

Fortunately for you, I'm here to take away many of your options.

XYZ Company   **12/2001–Present**

(It seems as if a lot of people work at this XYZ Co.)

Brief company description inserted here.

Director of Engineering   **5/2009–Present**

Listing of responsibilities and accomplishments.

Manager of Engineering   **5/2007–5/2009**

Listing of responsibilities and accomplishments.

Senior Staff Engineer   **12/2001–5/2007**

Listing of responsibilities and accomplishments.

ABC Company, Mountain View, CA   **10/1997–9/2001**

Brief company description inserted here.

Mechanical Engineer—Consumables

The above example is one way to do it, but it can be confusing. I prefer the dates of each position to be offset from the dates at each company, like this:

XYZ Company   **12/2001–Present**

Brief company description inserted here.

Director of Engineering   5/2009–Present

Listing of responsibilities and accomplishments.

Manager of Engineering   5/2007–5/2009

Listing of responsibilities and accomplishments.

Senior Staff Engineer   12/2001–5/2007

Listing of responsibilities and accomplishments.

ABC Company,
Mountain View, CA   10/1997–9/2001
Brief company description inserted here.
Mechanical Engineer-Consumables

See how much cleaner this looks, and how easy it is for the gatekeeper to glance at the resume and see the progression? Also note that this resume uses numbers for months, and that the dates following each *position* are in regular font, not bold. You want the dates for the companies to stand out and to be aligned. The dates for each position should be offset and unobtrusive. I have seen people do resumes with the dates on the left margin—and they look good—but it devours valuable space, so I prefer this option.

Now, let's talk about the gap in the work history. This person left ABC in 9/2001 and didn't start at XYZ until 12/2001. Many people would cover up the gap by listing years only. This person did it the right way. If you have a gap—leave it. *Show it.* **Shout it out.** It will earn you a red flag, but just one, and you can explain the gap to the gatekeeper when you get the interview. (Remember—along with the red flag, you also earn bonus points for being honest. Trust me; that goes a long way toward getting you the interview.)

Lying has no place in the resume, and resumes are where the lies usually rear their ugly heads, especially about dates. I've seen people leave out jobs, leave off dates, fudge dates, and outright lie about dates. Besides being *just not right,* when you lie about dates, it's too easy to get caught. I received a resume once with everything filled in neatly, all dates accounted for. I did some checking on Linked-in to see who else I knew that might have worked with this person, and I saw a recommendation from a person who said "worked with Bob at XYZ Company." I was puzzled. Bob's resume didn't show employment at XYZ Company. I did some digging, and, sure enough, Bob was at XYZ for about six months. He just "forgot" to mention it on his resume.

Needless to say, I didn't represent Bob. The sad thing is—and I checked this—his tenure at XYZ wasn't bad. He didn't get fired. He did nothing wrong. It was just one of those circumstances that didn't work out. Perfectly explainable to a prospective employer. Instead, Bob chose to hide it, and it cost him a shot at a good job.

One last point on dates. I bring this up because so many resumes list years only, not months. I know a lot of that comes from bad advice, and I hope that's the primary reason. But in case you're still thinking about it, read the statement below.

Then read it again.

- **If you don't put months on your dates of employment, you are *guilty until proven innocent*.**

Every gatekeeper and every headhunter I know gets suspicious when they see only years listed on a resume. If your resume shows 1997–2001, and then 2001 to present, the first thing *I* think is, "Did they leave in January 2001 and start the other job the following December?" It might be wrong to think like that, but it's a fact of life that gatekeepers do. If you don't put the months down, you're assumed guilty. Period. End of discussion. Resume trashed.

To Sum Up:

- Have your dates aligned, preferably to the far right.
- Show the dates you spent at each *company* in **bold.**
- Show the dates after each *position* offset to the left, not bold.
- *Do not* fudge on dates. Show both month and year on each one.
- Show any gaps in employment. Be prepared to explain those gaps, but *do not* try to cover them up.

Okay, let's move on to the Summary section.

Summary

EARLIER I TOLD YOU THAT SUMMARIES are unnecessary. You cringed. Don't deny it; I *know* you did. You probably thought, *Why did he say summaries are no good? Why should I leave them out?* Okay, fair question.

Let's Take a Look at Summaries

I know you feel like a summary is important, and why not? It *is* about you. I'm here to give you bad news. The summary is *not* important; in fact, *you* are not important—until you prove yourself. As far as the gatekeeper is concerned, you're no different than the hundreds of others in the "stack," and your summary *will not* change her mind. The only thing that *will* change her mind is a great cover letter combined with the perfect resume. And if you've been listening, you'll know that the summary section is not part of the perfect resume.

To Sum It Up

Summaries do *nothing*. They consist of you the candidate, the one trying to get in the castle, *telling* the gatekeeper how good you are.

Let's take a look at some real summaries:

SUMMARY OF QUALIFICATIONS:

I am a results-oriented seasoned Manager with extensive experience in Pre-Clinical And Clinical Development within Biopharmaceutical and Device industry. Successful track record of effectively directing Product Development, Global Regulatory (Us and Eu), Clinical, Quality and Marketing activities. I have demonstrated a keen ability to think and act Strategically, Tactically and Operationally, and in effectively managing collaborators and development partners. Self-starter, creative problem-solver and a valued team player.

Strong Organizational, Time Management, Risk Management and Leadership skills. Excellent interpersonal and Communication skills.

(Please note that almost none of the words this person capitalized should have been capitalized.)

Here's another one:

Summary: Seasoned professional with excellent presentation skills, extensive knowledge of the consumer electronics market, disk drive business, strategic account planning, team leadership/collaboration, and scientific innovation. I am seeking a position in a field that enables me to utilize my talents and strengths as technical director, scientific liaison, or product developer. I am very interested in working for a company that allows me to seek out new technology, new patents/intellectual properties, design and management of high profile launches and one where I can interact with clients to expand business and promote growth. General areas of interest include consumer electronics, disk drives, computers, telecommunications and network development. Fields of interest include research and development, consulting, marketing, sales, and business development.

(Can anyone tell me what this person wants to be when they grow up? I sure don't know.)

The Bottom Line

I know what you're thinking: *My summary is nothing like that. Mine is good. Mine is…*

Yes, I realize your summary is good. It's probably great. But to the gatekeeper they all sound the same. *Please* leave it off the resume. *Please?*

Education

As we construct our perfect resume, I'm putting Education near the top, because that's where it belongs. Many people bury Education at the bottom of the resume, forcing the gatekeepers to search for it. Don't do that!

Education is the one thing that *must* be on the resume, above all else. I don't necessarily recommend having a resume that consists of *only* education, but it has to be there, and it should be prominently displayed.

Now that we got that settled, here's how it should look:

Education: (Put it in bold, followed by a colon.)
If you have an advanced degree, put it first.

Ph.D., Chemistry	University of Maryland, College Park, MD
B.S., Chemistry	University of Illinois, Urbana-Champaign, IL

You could also do it like this:

University of Minnesota, Minneapolis, MN	MBA June 1994
University of Maryland, College Park, MD	BA, Biology May 1989

You can do it any number of ways as long as it's clean and doesn't take up too much space. I wouldn't put who your thesis advisor was, or who you did a post-doc with, or the names of your professors, even if they're famous. If relevant, address those things in a cover letter or in the interview.

You don't need to list *anything* other than the basics, and always put your education before work history.

Here's why:

Gatekeepers and headhunters, the two people who look at resumes most, want to see the education up front. If it isn't there, they look for it. They *stop* reading, and start searching.

Where is it? Does this person have a degree? Let me find it.

Hiding your education won't help. Gatekeepers won't read your resume until they find it. They'll hunt it down like a hound from hell.

Education is one of the few things headhunters and gatekeepers agree on. Even the most stubborn of the headhunters won't try convincing a gatekeeper to look at someone without a degree if the job description calls for one. Whether it's right or not is an issue for another book. It's a fact of life in the real world. So I'll say it one more time: EDUCATION GOES UP FRONT. PERIOD. NO ARGUMENT.

You'll notice I reverted to all caps. It's my opinion that you should *never* use all caps, but a few circumstances call for it: If you are a teenager; if you are *pretending* to be a teenager; and if you are trying to make a ridiculous point. This situation was the latter. (I have tried keeping my sarcasm under control, but occasionally it leaks out.)

No degree?

A special mention is in order. You may not have a degree, or you have one that doesn't meet the requirements in the job description. That might tempt you to hide your education at the end of the resume. Don't do it. Take that opportunity to sell yourself in the cover letter. Bring the issue up before they see it in the resume and counter your lack of experience with examples or reasons why they should consider you anyway.

When you handle the situation this way, it is disarming, sort of like your child coming home and telling you they did something bad today—before you found out about it. This approach takes the sting out, and it could make the difference. Every day people get hired for jobs they don't "fit" according to the requirements the job description called for. *You* can be one of them. Think about it this way: Bill Gates and Steve Jobs didn't have degrees. You might not be in the same situation, but you *can* get a job without a degree.

Personal

THERE IS NOTHING MORE PRIVATE than your personal life. Keep it that way. The only personal information the company needs should be at the top of the resume: your name, address, phone number, and email address. Nothing else. There should not be a *Personal* section.

Too Much Information

(Warning! Sarcasm ahead.)

I don't want to know your spouse's name. Or what religion you are, or that your son's name is Kip. I don't need to know that you have a Siamese or Burmese cat, or even a Bernese Mountain Dog. And I certainly don't need to know if you like Béarnaise sauce, unless you're applying for a chef's position.

A resume is all about the employer. It has nothing to do with you.

Let's take a look at some real examples from resumes:

PERSONAL DATA

Date of birth: March 28, 1961 (Could be *very* useful if I want to steal an identity. DOB's are also great for discrimination purposes.)

Spoken and written languages: Spanish, English (Appropriate if job calls for bi-lingual skills.)

Interests: Computers, baseball and family activities. (*Interested in computers and baseball. And family activities! Surely this will grab the gatekeeper's attention.*)

Non-professional activities:

Level 2 training as a little league baseball coach. (*Gatekeeper is getting excited.*)

Coach of a little league baseball team for 4 years. (*Really excited.*)

Manager of a minor hockey team for 3 years. (*Good Lord, what are we waiting for? Let's hire this person. Now!*)

The Bottom Line

Okay, I was a little extra sarcastic on the comments, but I did it to make a point—this kind of personal information doesn't belong on a resume. I understand it's important to you; it is to me also. But to the gatekeeper, it's *not* important, so leave those things off the resume.

Condensing the Resume

WRITING A RESUME IS DIFFICULT. You may be a good writer. You may be able to generate a report on yearly sales figures, write a proposal for entering a new market, a takeover, etc... But sit down in front of a keyboard to write a resume, and your mind goes blank. The polished writer inside you, the one that writes concise reports, the one who came home hours ago—is gone. You trash the first three drafts. You put in things that have no business being there. You stumble with the most common words. You forget how to be concise. Your resume is riddled with mistakes. All of the things you *don't* want.

Where to start?

Writing a resume is similar to writing a synopsis for a novel. A synopsis must condense about 100,000 words into two pages, and a resume must fit 5, or 10, or 30 years of experience into two pages. Both are a practice in perseverance, but it can be done, and it's fairly simple.

"How do I do that?" you ask.

By not being redundant. By being economical with words. Paring. Cutting. Using simple language. A lot of people think that a writer must use two-dollar words and write complicated, never-ending sentences to sound good. You don't. Trust me. I know.

Your resume is not a contest to see who can send the gatekeeper to the dictionary first or most often. Your resume should *never* send the gatekeeper to the dictionary. It will take up her time and aggravate her. And if she opens the dictionary, she'll likely find fault with the word you used.

Below are random examples I selected from several resumes. There are a number of words that I have seen frequently confused and misused, so I searched my database and came up with some examples. Since we're only dealing with resumes and cover letters in this book, we'll restrict the common problems to those found most often in those areas.

Resumes first. The following came from a vice president at a major company.

> Experience establishing, maintaining and managing joint research and development collaborations with other companies (e.g. cardiovascular projects with ABC Co. and XYZ Co.)

Did we need both *joint* and *collaborations?* Aren't those redundant? How about just saying:

> "Managed Cardiovascular R&D collaborations with ABC and XYZ."

Do we ever need to use the word *experience?* Sometimes. But if you *did* something, *took part in* something, developed a product, or marketed a product…didn't that give you experience?

Try this:

Go through your resume and look for the word *experience*. Every time you find it, take a hard look. Do you need it? Is there a better way to write that sentence?

How about "Experienced director of engineering"?

You could simply say: Director of Engineering.

Here's one I had to read twice

> "Originated, developed and implemented plans, policies and approaches for product development projects that led to the reduction of development cycle times of 20% to 50%."

This is not terribly confusing; however, I *did* have to read it twice to make sure I got what he was saying. Couldn't it have been said simpler? How about...

> "Developed plans which reduced development cycle times 20–50%."

That says it all, and it does so without making the gatekeeper read it twice. Plus, you save space.

The Bottom Line

Resist the urge to use big words. *Never* pull out a thesaurus. And make sure you're not being redundant. *Simple* is good when it comes to word choice.

Responsibilities

RESPONSIBILITIES TAKE UP A HUGE PART of most resumes, and that's unfortunate. I say *unfortunate*, because the space most people devote to responsibilities could be used much more effectively.

If you have a compelling reason to list responsibilities, follow these few rules:

- Keep it simple.

- Keep it short.

- Keep it relevant.

The only reason to even list responsibilities is to give the gatekeeper a sense of what your job involves, because it tells them nothing else. You can be responsible for anything, but it doesn't mean you did it well. My teenage son was *responsible* for keeping his room clean. Need I say more?

Another Tangent

Yes, I'm going off on another tangent, but this one deals with one of the most important parts of this book, so pay attention. If you don't listen to anything else, at least follow this advice: **Your resume must be tailored for *every* job you apply for. *Every* one.**

Imagine you ran a nice restaurant. You wouldn't serve the same meals to everyone, would you? You can set the tables the same, with plates and silverware and napkins. You can have the waiter pour a glass of water for each customer. But for the meal, you wait to find out what the customer wants before serving the food. Your resume is no different.

Certain things are set in concrete:

- Your name, address, and contact information
- Your education
- Where you worked
- Dates you worked
- Titles you held

But the rest of it needs to be tailored

I'm sure the chef at my favorite restaurant can cook all kinds of dishes, and I'm sure they're all good, but the only ones I care about are the seafood ravioli and the veal marsala.

When companies are looking to fill a position, they get into the hiring process with the same mindset. If they need someone to fix a broken development process and get new products out on time, they won't care that you won design awards or that your engineering department had the lowest turnover in the industry in the past ten years.

If you don't show them how you can get their products launched on time, you're not getting the job. Launching products on time is their problem; it's what needs fixing. Just like me sitting at the restaurant. If I can't get great seafood ravioli or veal marsala, I'm finding another place to eat. If the gatekeepers don't see the solution to their problem in you, they'll look at another candidate.

Now that we've covered that…

Let's look at the responsibilities section from a real resume

Responsibilities:

- Responsible for designing new mobile phone for burgeoning smartphone market.
- Responsible for extreme cost-cutting measures and yield improvements.

- Responsible for building world-class engineering group and championing design of revolutionary handset poised to be number one in market.

When I read something like this on a resume, the first thing I think is, *great,* this person was responsible for a lot—but did they accomplish any of it? **These questions immediately come to mind:**

- Did they get the phone designed, and how did it fare in the market?

- Were they able to cut costs and improve yields? By how much?

- Did this "revolutionary" handset even get to market, let alone take the number one spot?

This person would have been far better off translating those responsibilities into...

Accomplishments:

- Built an engineering team that designed, then launched, a new mobile phone for burgeoning smartphone market.

- Completed project one month ahead of schedule and 11% under budget.

- Launched product on time and captured 2% of worldwide market (12% more than projected) within first six months.

Final Note on Responsibilities

If you feel you absolutely have to include a few responsibilities on your resume, focus only on the key ones, the ones relevant to the job you're considering. Leave the insignificant ones off. You'll dilute your message and have less impact if you include minor things with big ones.

If you take a person's listing of their responsibilities at face value, they can be impressive. But only when you know the results do they become clear. A person can say that they were responsible for launching twenty products, but if they didn't launch any successfully, what good did that do?

The problem with resumes is that gatekeepers cannot interpret results by looking at a piece of paper, so candidates must provide gatekeepers with a way to get something meaningful from the resume. Responsibilities are *not* the way to do that. *Accomplishments* are. Before we get to that, though, we need to talk about punctuation. Yes, we really *need* to; punctuation is *that* important.

Punctuation, (:!-*%;—@"-#,), and Other Things

HAVE YOU EVER TRIED WATCHING a movie in the theater while people all around you are talking? Soon, you are so annoyed, you think of changing seats, or worse, you start listening to the conversations. In any case, you are distracted, and if the movie demands close attention, you'll miss something important.

Now imagine the *gatekeeper* who is reviewing your resume. She is cruising along, reading, getting into your background, when—wham—misplaced punctuation takes her out of reading mode. You don't want to distract the person reading your resume, especially when they're at your *Work History*.

The Work History part of your resume is the meat. It's where the gatekeepers focus their attention. It's where you *must* avoid anything that makes them stop reading. Remember, a resume's only purpose is to get you an interview. Just like you wouldn't go to an interview with stains on your suit or dirt under your fingernails, you don't want your resume to attract negative attention. It should be like a good interview suit—clean, the right size, simple yet professional. You want to avoid all mistakes, even with punctuation.

I know that most people don't pay much attention to punctuation, but a misplaced comma or misused colon is as much a mistake as a ~~mispelled~~ misspelled word. If you're going to do this resume right, learn to use punctuation, especially the dreaded semicolon. Many people don't know how to use a semicolon properly. The solution is simple: if you're not sure how, or when, to use the semicolon, either don't use it, or get your resume checked by someone who does know how to use it.

A *Quick* Lesson on Semicolons

There are three main circumstances when semicolons should be used. Despite what you might think, this isn't a grammar book, so I won't go into great detail.

1. To join two independent clauses that are closely related.

Example:

John rushed to the store; he had to get milk and bread, or his wife would kill him. (See how the second clause is closely tied to the first? John's life depends on that first clause. The second clause explains why John had to rush to the store.)

2. To separate lists that include commas.

Example:

John had fifteen minutes to do three things: fill the car with gas; stop and get milk, bread, and, perhaps a special treat; and get home before the new season of (take your pick) started.

3. To join two clauses using a conjunctive adverb.

(You see, that's why I didn't want to go into detail. Whenever I bring up conjunctive adverbs at parties everyone walks away.)

Example:

John had three things to do; however, he decided to take a shower before doing them.

You shouldn't have to worry about most of this. About the only time you should need a semicolon in your resume is for number 2, lists that include commas.

Capitalization:

Many people who write resumes have an inclination to capitalize damn near everything. Perhaps they think that by capitalizing words, those words, or the functions they represent, become more important; ergo, the person becomes more important. (Did I just use the word *ergo?* I did, didn't I? Smack me if I ever do that again. I will, in return, smack you if I see it on your resume. Or, if you're not around, I'll trash it. Fair enough?)

Back to capitalization

So THE CAPITALIZERS—Their Resumes End Up Looking Like This, instead of like this. It Makes It Damn Difficult To Read When The Wrong Words Are Capitalized. I Have Nothing Against Capitals, But You Should Only Use Them Where They Belong. AND DON'T EVER USE ALL CAPS. IT'S EVEN WORSE.

Compound Modifiers and Adjectives:

Don't be afraid! A *compound modifier* is simply a word you place a hyphen between to describe something. Examples of compound modifiers are *hands-on manager* or *high-volume manufacturing*.

I debated whether to bring this subject up, and the only reason I did was because compound modifiers are used so often on resumes. I believe they are used more there than anywhere else in writing.

The problem with compound adjectives or compound modifiers is that most people don't know when to use the hyphen and when not to. Resumes are riddled with mistakes, such as using compound adjectives where they don't belong, and not using them where they do. There *is* an upside to this. Most gatekeepers don't seem to mind mistakes made with compound modifiers. Perhaps it's because they don't know the rules of when to use them and when not to. That's understandable. The rules seem to change depending on who you ask and where you work.

There are a few general rules though, and they're easy to learn. If you follow even the primary one, you should be okay.

Compound Modifier Rules

Hyphenate a compound modifier when it comes *before* a noun, and don't hyphenate it when it comes *after* a noun. Here are some common compound adjectives/modifiers found on resumes:

- Hands-on
- High-volume
- High-precision
- Close-tolerance
- Leading-edge

Here are some real-world examples:

- They were in a long-term relationship. (In that sentence, I hyphenated *long-term* because it comes before the noun *relationship. Long-term* is a compound adjective that describes the word *relationship.*)
- Their relationship was long term. (No hyphen. I didn't hyphenate *long term* because it comes *after* the noun.)
- He was a hands-on manager.
- The product was produced in high volume.
- We need experience with high-volume, close-tolerance manufacturing.

Many rules govern the proper use of compound modifiers, especially when adverbs and phrasal adjectives are thrown in. If you want to learn more about this issue, consult a good style guide or go to a site like the wonderful one Grammar Girl maintains. The Grammar Girl has a great article on hyphens and compound modifiers and when to use them; in fact, Grammar Girl has great articles on just about every aspect of grammar. This is the link to her site: http://grammar.quickanddirtytips.com

If you're interested in learning more about semicolons, I did a short blog post about them. You can find it here: http://giacomo-giammatteo.com/2013/03/im-afraid-of/

Final Touch

WE ARE NEARING THE END OF THE JOURNEY. It's time to put the finishing touches on the perfect resume. As we've already discussed, accomplishments are the heart of the resume. That section is the *only* one that can actually help get you in the door; it's imperative that you make this area shine.

For those of you who like to think in sports terms, consider this: everything else on your resume is like playing defense; the only offense you have is the accomplishments section. (And your cover letter.)

One thing you need to do is use *impact* words. What are impact words? They are strong verbs and nouns. They are the *meat* of writing, just like the work history is the meat of your resume.

It's almost ironic that the place on your resume where you need the most powerful words tends to be the one place where all the weak words show up. Examples from actual resumes:

- Responsible for improving manufacturing 30%...
- Responsible for building new disk drive plant...
- Charged with increasing sales...
- Made improvements to...

These are *weak* statements, using *weak* words! Compare the above with this:

- Improved manufacturing by 30%...
- Built new disk drive plant...
- Increased sales...
- Improved...

One rule to remember is look for words ending in *ing*, because you can almost always replace them with an *action* verb that has real impact. Since resumes are written in past tense (or should be), your verbs should be powerful past-tense verbs. Most of them will end in *ed*.

Other Considerations

We've already talked about having no mistakes and leaving nothing to chance. When I say "no mistakes," I don't just mean typos. "No mistakes" can mean misuse of words, messing up formatting, not aligning the dates—*anything* that makes the resume less than perfect. A case in point is the use of bullets. In real life bullets can kill you, but when writing a resume they are your friends. Many people avoid bullets and lump everything together in one large paragraph. The following is an example taken from a real resume.

Director of Engineering and Product Development

Responsible for all technical aspects of development for complex telecommunication products. Responsible for product positioning, design concept, engineering verification, quality practices, supplier qualification and OEM customer qualifications. Responsible for recruiting, mentoring, managing and leading highly motivated engineers. Experience in management of rapid product development cycles.

Proven track record for on-time and on-budget product releases and experience in managing an entire product lifecycle. Improved manufacturing volume deliverables through enhanced forecasting and delivered three new products on time and under budget.

Achieved over 90% product acceptance rate of two new product releases by influencing the factory quality standards and engaging customer reception on quality criteria based on improved statistical process controls.

That's how it looked when it came in. Below is how it *should have* looked.

Director of Engineering and Product Development

Responsibilities:

Responsible for development, including product positioning, design concept, engineering verification, quality practices, supplier qualification and OEM customer qualifications.

Accomplishments:

• Recruited, mentored, managed, and led (not *lead*) team of highly-motivated engineers through rapid product development cycles.

• Delivered three new products on time and under budget.

• Improved manufacturing volume deliverables through enhanced forecasting.

• Achieved over 90% product acceptance rate of two new product releases by influencing the factory quality standards and engaging customer reception on quality criteria based on improved statistical process controls.

Remember: bullets are your friends. Use them.

If you use bullets for both responsibilities and accomplishments, you can make them different, but be consistent. So use • for responsibilities, for example, and use ♦ for accomplishments, or whatever you like best.

To sum up: [Pay attention, this might be the most important part of the book.]

- Your accomplishments should be bulleted.

- Your accomplishments should start with *action* words.

- Be concise. [Cut extra words.]

- Don't list too many; it dilutes the effect. [Top 2–3 responsibilities max, and 3–5 accomplishments.]

- List only those that are relevant to the job description. [Do not include trivial items or ones that are normal, everyday parts of your job.]

A special note about responsibilities and accomplishments.

We're going to take one more look at some of what this candidate had to say about their work history:

> "Responsible for product positioning, design concept, engineering verification, quality practices, supplier qualification and OEM customer qualifications. Responsible for recruiting, mentoring, managing and leading highly motivated engineers. Experience in management of rapid product development cycles."

If you are a director of engineering, of course you are responsible for recruiting, mentoring, managing, etc... No need to tell us that.

Almost lost in the shuffle was this gem:

- "Delivered three new products on time and under budget."

Now *that's* important. This candidate would have been far better off if they had eliminated most of the responsibilities and even some of the accomplishments. This is what I was talking about when I said not to dilute your achievements.

When you include duties that are expected of you—the normal everyday duties—it's like your kid coming home and saying to his mother, "I got to the bus on time again. And I didn't miss any classes. I finished all my homework. Oh, and I saved a boy from drowning on the way home."

"That's nice, dear. Wash up. Dinner's almost ready."

"Did you hear me, Mom? I saved a boy from drowning."

"You did *what!*"

See how that one major accomplishment got lost in the exchange? That can happen with a resume, too. The difference is, you don't get a chance to say, "Did you hear me, Mom?"

With a resume, you get one shot. That's it. Make it count.

Ready to move on? I think you're almost ready.

Company Descriptions

MOST WORK HISTORY SECTIONS START OUT LIKE THIS:

WORK HISTORY:

XYZ Company,
Redwood City, CA   **10/2005–Present**

Director of Research and Development

Responsibilities:

Stop!

If your resume looks like this, you're missing a golden opportunity—*the company description.*

Remember, most resumes are screened by either headhunters or gatekeepers before they ever get to the hiring manager. As talented and magnificent as gatekeepers and headhunters are, we are not experts in every discipline, and we don't know all of our competitors or the products that may be similar to the ones our company makes. A brief company description could make a huge difference in how your resume is viewed.

Let's assume the gatekeeper works at a new biotech company getting into the market for infectious diseases. The following is a good example of why a company description might help.

XYZ Company,

Redwood City, CA   10/2005–Present

Seven-year old biopharmaceutical company focusing on the development and commercialization of new anti-bacterial and anti-fungal drugs for the prevention or treatment of serious infectious diseases.

That isn't much. It takes up a few lines on the resume. But to the gatekeeper or the headhunter reading this, it immediately shows them the relevant experience. As soon as they read "anti-bacterial and anti-fungal drugs for the prevention or treatment of serious infectious diseases," they know your background is a fit, at least from the specific sector of their industry. Now they'll read your resume with a little more care. They *peruse* it instead of *skimming* it.

Now look closer at that description. That little blurb tells us a *lot* more than the market the company is in. It is a seven-year-old biopharmaceutical company, and the candidate has been there since 2005. That tells us she's been there since the beginning, has experienced the growth and problems of a small-company environment, and has *survived*. To a new company like the one the gatekeeper works for, that's important information. Even more reason for her to carefully review this resume.

Please note that I changed the font, the size of the font, and the line spacing for the description. It provides contrast while reducing space. Sometimes the contrast helps draw attention, and that's a good thing. It also breaks up the monotony, so when the gatekeeper is finished reading the description, she moves on to the job title with a little freshness.

Some people prefer the company description be in italics. I think either way works fine, so go with what you like.

We'll pick up again in the next chapter, incorporating this into your final resume.

Note: Some people advise leaving company descriptions out of the resume. They say gatekeepers will look up the information if they don't know it. All I can say is—they don't know Rose. Trust me. A gatekeeper *won't* look anything up. If it isn't on the resume, it won't register.

Your Fixed Resume

John Doe

2416 Job Hunters Cove, San Diego, CA 92121

Cell# (858) 555-5555 Home (858) 555-4545

johndoe@someserver.com

Education:

University of Someplace Important, Bend in the Road, PA
MBA   June 1997

Less Prestigious College, Nowhere, New Mexico
BA, Chemistry   May 1983

Language Skills: Fluent in Russian

Work History:

**I Finally Made It Corp.,
San Diego, California**   **7/2003–Present**
*A $15 billion publicly-traded company which develops, manu-
factures and commercializes consumer, industrial and healthcare
products globally.*

Director of Sales

Responsibilities:
- Accountable for $300 million in revenue and $11 million in expenses.
- Provide overall sales direction to a team of 7 regional managers and 42 sales representatives.

Accomplishments:
- Implemented Russian Culture Awareness program for new sales reps, increasing share of Russian market from 7% to 24% in less than two years.
- Increased sales from $89 million to $300 million, growing above industry average with top-line growth rate of 8%.
- Ranked as #1 director 7 out of 8 years.
- Developed new incentive program, which drove sales to record high, while keeping expenses 9% below budget.

I'm Almost There Corp.,
San Diego, California   1/1999–7/2003
A $210 million publicly-traded company that developed, manufactured and commercialized high-quality medical products.

Director of Sales   9/2000–7/2003
Director of Marketing   1/1999–9/2000

Responsibilities:
- Accountable for $75 million in revenue and $8 million in expenses. Managed 70-person sales team of 20 direct reps and 50 manufacturer reps.
- Accountable for new product development, strategic planning, P/L for manufacturing, and all medical business development. Led the marketing/business development staff of 8 for medical business unit.

Accomplishments:
- Developed and implemented business plan for market expansion into the alternate care and consumer markets, resulting in a 35% increase in sales, including a $10 million dollar contract from national chain.
- Hired and trained 12 new sales reps. All but one met or exceeded quota for the year.

Thought I'd Made It Inc.,
Irvine, California   5/1997–1/1999
A $2 billion publicly-traded company which develops, manufactures and commercializes devices related to in-vitro diagnostic systems in the laboratory disciplines of clinical chemistry, hematology, special chemistry, robotics automation and immunodiagnostics.

Region Manager   10/1998–1/1999
Area Manager   5/1997–10/1998

Accomplishments:
- Hired two new sales reps and broke all sales records for S. California region.
- Negotiated largest account in region's history—$10 million in revenue for a new diagnostic system.
- Managed six sales reps, all of whom exceeded quota by more than 30%.

What a Mistake Inc.,
Parsippany, NJ   1/199–5/1997
A $90 million company which specialized in the development, manufacture, commercialization and support of in-vitro diagnostic systems.

Region Sales Manager   12/1994–5/1997
National Accounts Manager   1/1993–12/1994

Responsibilities:
Accountable for $15 million in revenue and sales team of 8 people.

Accomplishments:
- Recognized as Region Manager of the year in both 2006 and 2007, with 15% growth per year.
- Developed the strategic direction and managed the tactical implementation of the company's program, including achieving 30% sales growth with government, corporate and national accounts.
- Developed corporate identity program, contract management systems and pricing policies for corporate accounts.

Let's Analyze This

I know I have preached about not including much in the way of responsibilities, but the way it's done on this resume is *exactly* how it should be done. Look at the first job—Director of Sales. John Doe tells us that he is accountable for $300 million in revenue and $11 million in expenses, and that he is responsible for a team of 7 regional managers and 42 sales reps. That gives us the information we need to analyze his accomplishments, which, by the way, he does perfectly—by quantifying them.

Take a look:

- Implemented Russian Culture Awareness program for new sales reps, increasing share of Russian market from 7% to 24% in less than two years.

- Increased sales from $89 million to $300 million, growing above industry average with top-line growth rate of 8%.

- Ranked as #1 director 7 out of 8 years.

- Developed new incentive program, which drove sales to record high, while keeping expenses 9% below budget.

This is the way to combine responsibilities and accomplishments: one complements the other. The responsibilities provide the scope of the job, and the accomplishments show what you did.

Okay, you're getting there. This resume is *good*. I think it's almost ready.

A special note about recent graduates:

You don't have much work history, and your resume may look like the Saharan Desert, which makes it even more important that you follow the rules in this book, especially the ones dealing with cover letters.

A gazillion people graduate from college each year, and all of them are looking for jobs. Every one of them has the same kind of resume you do. Their GPAs are different; their schools are different; their fields of study, etc... but only *you* can make the real difference—and you do that with the cover letter. The cover letter is your chance to get someone's attention. Don't waste it.

That said, this is another area where common sense comes into play. If you have followed the suggestions in this book and filled out all of the details in your resume, and you find yourself staring at a half-page, it wouldn't hurt to include additional information in the education section. Just don't get carried away, and try to make it relevant.

Examples:

- Instead of simply stating that you were a member of the chess club, *show* that you joined because you enjoyed stimulating, analytical challenges, and mention how that will be an advantage in the engineering position you're applying for.

- Turn that stint on the gymnastics team into a reason why that same competitive drive will help you succeed in the sales position you're applying for.

The key is for *you* to take the initiative. *Do not* leave it up to the person reviewing your resume to analyze why you might have played chess or football, or why you joined the drill team or competed in gymnastics. Address these things in your cover letter— as they apply to the job—and have them on your resume as the backup.

Final note:

If the school you graduated from ranks highly in your field, make a note of it. The gatekeepers can't know all of the schools, and you don't want them assuming that the one you attended isn't a good one simply because they don't recognize it. Until a few years ago, I didn't realize that the Indian Institute of Technology had such a good reputation. Now that I know, seeing IIT on a resume stands out, and I pay closer attention.

Lies

BEFORE SENDING YOUR RESUME OUT, check for lies.

Lie: definitions from the dictionary.

1. A false statement deliberately presented as being true. A falsehood.

2. Something meant to deceive or give a wrong impression.

3. To present false information with the intention of deceiving.

4. To convey a false image or impression.

Lies—the father of all sins

I'll make a lot of exceptions for mistakes on resumes. I'll forgive a few misused words; I'll look over a spelling error or two; I'll even read past (not *passed*) objectives and summaries. I will *not*, however, overlook a lie, whether it be a bald-faced lie[2] or one of omission.

You wouldn't believe the number of lies we find on resumes. People lie about education, about work history, about anything. If you have a degree from one of the so-called "Universities" that basically "sell" you a degree, don't list it. Don't buy it to begin with. You're far better off listing no degree than being caught faking one. And trust me—the gatekeepers and headhunters know about those fake degrees, and they recognize many of them.

They also know when they *don't* recognize a school. If I see a resume with an MS degree in Quality Engineering from "XYZ" University in New York or Boston, and if I don't remember seeing that university before, I look it up. If I can't find it, guess what. No, the resume doesn't go to the trash. Not yet. I'm going to ask you about it first, but if you can't show me that the degree is real *then* it goes into the trash.

A note to all of you without degrees: Having no degree does make it tough. Damn tough. But many successful, even famous, executives have no degree: Steve Jobs, Bill Gates, and Michael Dell, to name only a few.

Remember, not having a degree is nothing to be ashamed of. Lying is.

There are many kinds of lies:

- Lying by omission on dates
- Lying by job title
- Leaving companies you worked for off the resume
- Misrepresenting facts
- Lying about why you left the job—if you were fired, say so, but not on the resume.

Some candidates have told me they received advice to leave dates off the resume if they didn't represent continuous employment. Other advice suggested hiding gaps. One resume book advises people to use a different format of resume to cover up jobs they don't want to show, or to hide gaps in employment. Anyone giving this advice should be ashamed of themselves. I'll state it one more time. Do not *lie* on your resume. NEVER. EVER. It's not worth it. It doesn't pay off.

You'll know if it's wrong. You'll likely get this sick feeling in your gut if you try to cover something up. You will *know* you shouldn't do it. If you get that feeling, listen to it.

So before you send out your resume, go through it and look specifically for the fine elements of truth.

- Are all of the dates correct?
- Are there any omissions?
- Are your titles all correct?

- How about your responsibilities?
- Accomplishments:
  - Did you exaggerate any?
  - Did you make them look a *little* bit better than they were?
  - Did you *really* increase sales by 20%, or was it 18%?

I will end this section with a famous quote by a former president.
"I am not a crook."

Spellcheckers

I KNOW YOU'RE EXCITED. Your resume is perfect. You're ready to send it. You *want* that interview.

STOP! DO NOT HIT SEND! DO NOT PASS GO! (I play a lot of Monopoly.)

You cannot send your resume until you check it again. Yes, I know, you've checked it five times already. Let's do it one more time. I can almost hear you saying, "But my spellchecker said it was okay."

I'm going to let you in on a secret—spellcheckers are *dangerous*. They're like having a guard dog who only guards against certain intruders. There are far too many words they won't catch—like homophones—yet we feel safe and secure with our spellcheckers. They put us in a comfort zone where we think they're doing their job. They don't. They won't. They will embarrass you. Humiliate you. Make you look careless. Is that what you want? Are you willing to risk mistakes, entrust your resume, potentially your *future*, to a spellchecker?

If I haven't convinced you to turn off your spelling checker yet, please read the following poem. Many people know it as "The Spell Checker Poem," but the real work is titled "Candidate for a Pullet Surprise." It was written by Jerrold H. Zar, and published in *The Journal of Irreproducible Results*, v39 #1, January/February 1994, p 13, and v45 #5–6, 2000, p 20.

I have included parts of it here, and the full poem can be viewed on the publisher's website: http://www.jir.com/pullet.html

Candidate for a Pullet Surprise

I have a spelling checker,
It came with my PC.
It plane lee marks four my revue
Miss steaks aye can knot sea.

Eye ran this poem threw it,
Your sure reel glad two no.
Its vary polished in it's weigh.
My checker tolled me sew.

A checker is a bless sing,
It freeze yew lodes of thyme.
It helps me right awl stiles two reed,
And aides me when eye rime.
......
To rite with care is quite a feet
Of witch won should bee proud,
And wee mussed dew the best wee can,
Sew flaw's are knot aloud.
......

Okay, now that you've digested that, let's get ready. Go to a quiet place. Don't pour any wine. Put on your glasses if you wear them. Read carefully. Look at *each* word. See if it fits. Is it the right word? Is it necessary? Check everything. Once you're satisfied that nothing is wrong, take a deep breath—and turn *on* the spellchecker. Make one pass with it, see if it finds any mistakes.
....
...
Okay, done?
At the count of three—TURN OFF THE DAMN SPELL-CHECKER.

Now peruse that resume, scrutinize it. At the risk of using a cliché—go through it with a fine-tooth comb. After you're done, have a friend go through it. *Insist* they find a mistake. Offer to *pay* them to find a mistake. I just got an idea: offer your teenage son/daughter *money* if they find a mistake. I can't imagine them passing up both money *and* the opportunity to make a parent look bad. Trust me; they'll find a mistake. If they don't find one, you're finally ready to send your resume out.

Wait! Have you written a cover letter?

Cover Letters—Your Chance to Shine (or look like an ass)

COVER LETTERS. WHEW! You're halfway done.

"What?" you say. *"Halfway?* We finished the resume; all we have left is the cover letter."

All we have left is the cover letter? I can't believe what I'm hearing.

Listen, I know that most people don't use cover letters. That should make you happy. Why? Because that gives you an edge. Using a cover letter is like a guy taking flowers to his girlfriend's mother on the first date. And yes, they *are* that powerful.

The cover letter is *it.* Sending off that resume without a cover letter is like leaving the house without your cell phone. You just don't do it. Period. You *do not* send a resume without a cover letter. In fact, if you're working with a headhunter, *insist* that they allow you to write a cover letter for *each* position they submit you for. That last statement is important because your cover letter must be tailored to a specific position. There's not much worse than a generic cover letter.

Broken down to its simplest forms, we can look at it this way: every decision, or most decisions, in life are problem/solution related.

- Car breaks down and need to get a new one? The one you pick will be determined by your specific needs. If you have six kids to haul to soccer practice every week, the solution won't be a sports car.

- Got a carpet to clean? The kind of stain will determine the cleaning solution you buy.

- Have a medical problem? You're not going to a podiatrist if you have a heart problem. I would hope you'd choose a cardiologist.

A job opening is no different. When a company has an opening, they have a problem, and the job description is the key to figuring out the solution to that problem.

Earlier I said a resume had one job—to get you an interview. Actually, the resume is better suited for another job—to keep you out of the trash. The resume would be better off letting the cover letter be the point man, the seller, the closer. Think of the resume as customer support/sales support. Back there, ready with data, dates, job titles, and all of those things a gatekeeper can refer to as your cover letter excites her. *That*, my friends, is the perfect combination. And it is one few people take advantage of.

Nailing the Interview

Up to this point, we've talked about how to avoid mistakes. What not to include. How to present yourself on paper. But the cover letter is the key to the city. Use it.

Remember, when a company has a job to fill, what they really have is a *problem*. Your job is to offer them a *solution*. Find out what their problems/challenges are, and *show* them how you can solve them.

- Is the company having quality problems?

  - *Show* how you improved quality at the last place you worked.

- Are they experiencing high turnover?

  - *Show* what you did to stabilize employment and reduce turnover.

- Slow sales?

  - *Show* how you increased sales by X percent in your last two positions.

The first candidate to do this effectively will get the job offer. In case you missed it, the key word in those statements was *show*. You cannot *tell* on a resume, or walk into an interview and *tell* them that you're the answer to their problems. You must *show* them, through what you have done in the past, that you are the one who will be able to do it again—for them.

Companies don't bet on long shots, especially when it comes to hiring. They take the people who are likely to come in first, time and time again. If you want the job offer, you need to be the favorite in this horse race.

More Mistakes

A cover letter opens up wonderful opportunities, but it is also where mistakes seem to appear most often. In a cover letter, write in complete sentences; your thoughts must be fluid, your points valid. In other words, *show* the gatekeeper that you're capable of communicating using the written word. This is both a chance to shine and a pitfall awaiting an unwary victim. Remember the moat we talked about, the one surrounding the castle? This moat is filled with sharp spikes and ravenous piranha. If you slip up here, the gatekeeper will never see your resume.

The cover letter is where I see a tremendous misuse of words, and, since it's the first thing the gatekeeper looks at, that's not good.

Let's cover some of the most common mistakes:

A/an—A mistake I often see is the misuse of the indefinite articles *a* and *an*. The rules are simple, yet people often get them confused.

You use *a* in front of a word beginning with a consonant *sound*, regardless of spelling. So it would be *a* fox, *a* dog, *a* university (the *u* makes a *y* sound), and yes, it would be *a* historic event. (It is not *istoric*, but *historic*, with an *h* sound.)

Use *an* in front of words beginning with a vowel *sound*, again, regardless of spelling. So it would be *an* elephant, *an* ostrich, *an* antelope, and *an* honor. (In the word *honor*, the *h* is not pro-nounced.) Words beginning with *h* and *u* seem to be the ones that confuse most people.

Adverse/averse—I have also seen this quite often on cover letters: "I am not adverse to…"

Many people confuse "adverse" and "averse." The difference is fairly easy to remember. If you are using the word *to* after it, use *averse*.

So if someone writes, "I am not *averse to* rolling up my sleeves and doing hands-on work," they would use *averse to* not *adverse*.

I am going to interject yet another opinion here. Remember how we spoke of simple words versus two-dollar words. *Averse* might not be a two-dollar word, but you can achieve the same effect (not *affect*) using a simpler phrase. So instead of saying, "I am not *averse to* rolling up my sleeves and doing hands-on work," it would be a lot (not *alot*) cleaner by saying, "I don't mind rolling up my sleeves and doing hands-on work." Trust me, the gate-keeper will be impressed.

Assure/ensure/insure—These words are frequently found on resumes and demand to be included. This threesome falls into the *worst offenders* category. Many people use these words inter-changeably, and, according to most grammarians, erroneously. They all have the general meaning of making the outcome of a particular circumstance certain; however, there *are* distinct differences.

I often see statements like this on a resume:

"*Insured* delivery of products on time and under budget by…"

The proper way to state that would be "*Ensured* delivery…"

To break it down further:

Assure is typically used to *assure* someone/some living thing, of the outcome. Example: You might *assure* your boss that the project will get done on time and under budget.

Ensure is used more for things than people. So to *ensure* the project gets done on time, you hire more people and secure additional resources.

Insure, in its pure form, refers to money or insurance. So I *insured* the project for $10 million dollars in case of accidents.

Here's the easiest way to remember the distinction between these words:

Assure is used for people. (You can make an *"ass"* of yourself if you promise your boss something and don't deliver.)

Ensure is used for things.

Insure deals with money/insurance.

Alright/all right—Many people think that *alright* is *all right*, but a lot of others disagree, and to those who disagree, using *alright* is like using *ain't*. Why bother when so much is at stake, use *all right*.

Alot/a lot—This is an easy one. *Alot* is *not* a word. It is always *a lot*—two words.

Anxious/eager—Some people use anxious and eager as if they were the same word, with similar meanings. It is becoming more acceptable in common usage (which is a damn shame), but there *are* differences—*meaningful* differences. "Anxious" stems from the word *anxiety*. The Merriam-Webster dictionary defines anxiety as:

a: an abnormal and overwhelming sense of apprehension and of fear often marked by such physical symptoms as tension, tremor, sweating, palpitation, and increased pulse rate

Most all dictionaries cite examples of anxious being used in the sense of being *eager*, but I prefer to follow the more formal line. This is from the American Heritage Dictionary of the English Language: "Anxious has a long history of use as a synonym for eager, but many usage writers prefer that anxious be used only when its subject is worried or uneasy about the anticipated event."

Usage examples:

I am *eager* to see my fiancée; she has been away for two weeks. But I am *anxious* about meeting her family.

Notice that *eager* is usually coupled with *to* and *anxious* goes with *about*.

So you wouldn't tell the gatekeeper you are *anxious to* come for an interview. You might actually be *anxious about* interviewing, but tell the gatekeeper you are *eager to* come for an interview. That will mean more to her.

Lead/led—Been there. Done that. If you need to review this, it can be found in the *Purpose of a Resume* section.

Peeked/Peaked/Piqued—If you're going to use one of these words, make certain you use the right one.

> *Peeked*, is used for things like "He *peeked* around the corner to get a look at the new neighbor in her bikini." (I'm *not* referring to me. No way. Not ever.)

> Electricity usage *peaked* during August, typically the hottest month in Texas. (I can vouch for that.) This can also refer to the peak of a mountain.

> Dear Gatekeeper: my interest was *piqued* by reading an article on the company's new product. (Ah! There's the definition we were searching for.)

Unique

I often see phrases such as *very unique*.

I hope you know what's wrong with that. Nothing is very unique. There are no degrees to unique. Its meaning is absolute. Nothing can be *really* unique, *quite* unique, or *very* unique. Other words fall into this same category: equal, infinite, perfect, complete. Something is either unique, or it isn't. Something is equal, perfect, infinite, complete—or it isn't. It's like being dead. Either you are or you aren't. You can't be *very* dead.

Now that we have dealt with some of the big offenders, let's move on. The focus of the cover letter starts, and ends, with the job description. Get that description out. Set it on the desk/table beside you and highlight the key challenges and requirements. Now, let's get busy.

Keywords

BEFORE WE START, IT'S IMPORTANT to remember that companies demand that resumes be perfect, but companies' job descriptions are far from perfect. Many are rehashed versions of ones written years ago, and those that aren't are often thrown together in a hurry with little thought given to the content. They're typically filled with never-ending lists of responsibilities simply to take up space. Fluff for the sake of fluff.

For this example, we'll use a real job description, warts and all. This is a mediocre job description—better than most, worse than many, but it conveys the key points, so it will suffice. Besides, we're not here to pick apart job descriptions; that's for another book.

Remember to read the description and select what you feel are the most important points. Once you've done that, address those points in your cover letter.

How are you supposed to tailor your resume to a poorly-written job description?

You have to work with what's provided. Identify the important requirements then write a cover letter to show that you can do the job and solve their problem. Make sure the resume backs you up, showing where and when you got that experience. Now that you have that straight (not *strait*), let's take a look at how to decipher that job description.

Identify Key Points

If the job description is written well, the most important items will be at the top of the list. Even on poorly written ones, the top typically contains key items, so you almost can't go wrong focusing some of your efforts there.

Look for strong verbs

Later I'll mention *impact words*. The words you're looking for in the job description should be the same—*if* the description was written well. The verbs to look for usually refer to action items, so words like *direct, manage, launch, build,* and *develop* are all focus points. The words you can usually ignore are ones such as *monitor, evaluate, assist,* and *coordinate*. (Depending on the type of position.) These words seldom fall into the absolute-requirements category when a gatekeeper is considering a candidate.

Now that you've found the strong verbs, it's time to identify the all-important nouns that follow them

Why?

Because these nouns will not only tell you what the company is really looking for, but they also serve as the words a company will use for electronic screening. Yes, it's a new age, and most companies—like it or not—use some form of screening software to muddle through the huge number of resumes they get. This software is set up to scan for certain words—usually the important nouns found in the job description. These tremendously important nouns serve several purposes for you, so don't take them lightly. They will

- Identify what you need to address in your cover letter.
- Tell you what accomplishments to focus on in your resume.
- Ensure that your resume will be picked up by the screening software.

How to Identify Keywords

Once you find the verbs, ask "What?"

Below is the job description we're using, so let's look at the responsibilities and requirements to find those keywords.

Job Description: Vice President and Head of Global Sales & Marketing—XYZ Company.

Responsibilities:

- Direct and manage sales and marketing strategies to drive worldwide sales and expand company's presence in global market.

- Evaluate market opportunities and conditions with focus on identifying new product opportunities.

- Recommend plans, policies and/or structural changes to grow and expand company's product lines.

- Develop and implement short-term and long-term business and marketing strategies to increase worldwide revenues and profitability.

- Develop annual sales forecast in line with company's overall growth plan and implement effective strategies and tactics to achieve targets.

- Collaborate with the Design Core Team on the development of new products and services to meet the needs of the market.

- Monitor and analyze trends, emerging opportunities, and risks and threats, keeping all stakeholders informed of market activities that could affect the organization.

- Assist with the development of standards, calibrators, controls, future diagnostic assays, and clinical tests.

- Establish and manage effective marketing communication, including regular interaction and meetings with distributors, key customers, and potential customers.

- Work with the CEO and the other executive team members to identify and develop strategic alliances and business-development opportunities.

Requirements:

- 10+ years of managerial level experience in strategic sales and marketing of similar products.
- Experience in business-development activities, including personal involvement and experience with strategic planning and market analysis.
- International experience with a good understanding of global business development and a technical understanding of molecular diagnostics.
- Fluency in Russian or other European languages would be preferred.
- Excellent analytical skills with the ability to present complex data and information in a form that is engaging and tailored to the audience.
- Excellent communication skills with an ability to train employees.
- BA/BS degree.
- Location: Philadelphia, PA.

In this example, the first few responsibilities use the verbs *direct, manage, drive, expand, evaluate, recommend,* and *develop.* Of those verbs, the ones most likely to be important are *direct, manage, expand,* and *develop.*

Now let's look for the nouns, which is fairly simple. All you do is ask "What?" following each verb. For example:

- "Direct or manage what?" = **sales and marketing strategies**
- "Drive what?" = **worldwide sales**
- "Expand what?" = **presence in global markets**

When we get to the word "develop," you'll see two things listed. The first deals with increasing worldwide revenues and profitability, while the second deals with sales forecasts and achieving targets. This is where the common sense comes into play. The first listing seems more important, so address that one.

Under the requirements section, you'll notice they ask for "international experience with a good understanding of global business development." They wouldn't ask for international experience on a whim, which means it's probably a key point. As far as the next item—fluency in a different language—when a company says something is *preferred*, it usually means they don't expect to get it, but it would be nice. If you have experience in an area they list as preferred, be sure you mention it; that could move you to the top of the pile.

To summarize:

- Focus on items at the top of the list.
- Look for the impact verbs—the important nouns will follow them.
- Use common sense.

Job Description

NOW THAT YOU'VE GONE THROUGH the job description and highlighted a few key areas, let's draft your cover letter. Be careful; you don't want to make this a short story. Cover letters, like resumes, must be concise. Try to keep them to one page. Exceed that only if absolutely necessary. With what you've learned about concise writing, that shouldn't be difficult.

Dear Gatekeeper: I know we are referring to her as the gatekeeper, but in real life, get the person's name and verify that you have it spelled correctly, with the correct title. (More on that in the next chapter.) Make sure you address the letter formally. This isn't the time to be chummy. Refer to the job by its title. If you have a job number/reference, use that.

Dear Gatekeeper:

I noticed you are looking for a vice president of sales and marketing, with an emphasis on increasing sales in the international market. (Please note that job titles are not capitalized.) That piqued my curiosity. I have a successful track record as a director in sales and marketing for Fortune 500 companies as well as mid-sized enterprises and start-ups.

Regarding international sales, I am not only fluent in Russian, but I implemented a Russian Culture Awareness program for new sales reps, which more than tripled our share of the market in less than two years. The program was so successful, it now forms the basis of training for all new foreign markets.

I noticed in the job description you asked for "a good understanding of global business development and a technical understanding of molecular diagnostics."

I have found that global business development is done best by those who understand the culture of the countries they are dealing with. I have lived in thirteen countries in Europe and Asia, and have demonstrated a keen understanding of their cultures. While I do not have a strong technical grasp of molecular diagnostics, that has never been an issue in the past.

One thing not mentioned on the resume was a co-promotion partnership I initiated with a major pharmaceutical company in Germany which resulted in a 50% increase in recommendations for our products by doctors, increasing sales by 29% in the first year. In addition, I have switched segments of the industry three times and have been successful in each of them. I am confident I can do the same for you.

As far as location, Philadelphia presents no problem.

I am eager to speak with you about this opportunity and to demonstrate how I can help XYZ Company achieve its goals.

Sincerely,

Me

Let's take a breather and go back through that chapter. Cover letters are so important we need to spend a little extra time on them.

A Quick Analysis
of the Cover Letter

I'VE SEEN EXPERTS ADVISE CANDIDATES to write a casual cover letter. All I can say is *nonsense*. I've never seen anyone disqualified for "doing it right." When it comes to business writing, you can't go wrong with formal. You should address the cover letter as if your job depended on it—it might. The cover letter needs to be professionally written and addressed. Below is a standard format.

Your Name
Your Address
Your City, State, Zip Code
Your Phone Number
Your Email

Date

Name
Title
Company/Organization
Address
City, State, Zip Code

Dear Mr./Ms. Last Name:

Many positions don't list a name of who to send the resume to; it's just an email address to an "admin," or generically to human resources. If that's the case, you have a little work to do. The easiest way is often the direct approach—call the company and ask. Nine times out of ten, the receptionist will give you the answer. Be sure you get the correct spelling, and correct title. And please, double check. Letters often sound alike on the phone, so an "s" and an "f" or a "b" and "v," can easily be mixed up.

When you feel you have the correct name, check again. Go to LinkedIn and verify the name and title. If they're not on LinkedIn, try the company website, assuming the person is at a high enough level to be listed there.

I spent a lot of time on just the name, but I did it for a reason. Not much will earn you a red flag faster than addressing the resume/cover letter to the wrong person, or to the right person with their name spelled wrong.

Your cover letter should be brief, but not too brief. Half a page is probably not enough, but one page should be fine, because you're only going to have three sections. The first is the *Introduction*, followed by the *Sell*, and ending with the *Close*. Keep the *introduction* and the *close* to one short paragraph. The *sell* you can expand, as you'll need to address at least a few key points of the job description.

Cover letters need to have just as much, if not more, attention paid to them as the resume. And one item to note—don't ever say you're the best candidate, or the ideal candidate. You don't know that. It will make you sound like an ass. Now let's go back and analyze what you said to the gatekeeper.

Dear Gatekeeper:

I noticed you are looking for a vice president of sales and marketing, with an emphasis on increasing sales in the international market. That piqued my curiosity. I have a successful track record as a director in sales and marketing for Fortune 500 companies as well as mid-sized enterprises and start-ups.

> *This is a good introduction. You mentioned the job correctly, and stated that you understood what they were looking for. You also mentioned your relevant experience.*

Regarding international sales, I am not only fluent in Russian, but I implemented a "Russian Culture Awareness" program for new sales reps, which more than tripled our share of the market in less than two years. The program was so successful it now forms the basis of training for all new foreign markets.

> *Great lead into the sell. You picked out what appeared to be one of the key requirements and showed them that not only are you proficient in this area, but that it wasn't a fluke. Your program was so successful it was adopted by your company as the gold standard.*

I noticed in the job description you asked for "…a good understanding of global business development and a technical understanding of molecular diagnostics."

I have found that "global business development" is done best by those who understand the culture of the countries they are dealing with. I have lived in thirteen countries in Europe and Asia, and have demonstrated a keen understanding of the cultures. While I do not have a strong technical grasp of molecular diagnostics, that has never been an issue in the past.

> *Another good selling point. You countered a potential weakness with a statement that shows you understand the issue, but you feel you can overcome that, because you've done it before, and not much is more powerful than having done it before— successfully.*

One thing not mentioned on the resume was a co-promotion partnership I initiated with a major pharmaceutical company in Germany which resulted in a 50% increase in recommendations for our products by doctors, increasing sales by 29% in the first year. In addition, I have switched segments of the industry three times and been successful in each of them. I am confident I can do the same for you.

> *This is gold! You're showing them something significant that is not mentioned on the resume. This isn't fluff. This is the kind of information that will make the gatekeeper think, what else isn't shown on the resume? A little curiosity can go a long way to getting you an interview.*

As far as location, Philadelphia presents no problem.

I am eager to speak with you about this opportunity, and to demonstrate how I can help "XYZ Company" achieve its goals.

> *The close is simple and effective. I like the soft sell when it comes to closing for an interview. The time to get more aggressive is the offer stage. Here you countered any possible questions about location by mentioning it was no problem, and then you expressed interest, and confidence by stating you were eager to demonstrate how you can help them achieve their goals.*

Resumes and cover letters are the one-two punch that will get you the job you want.

The goal of your cover letter it to leave the gatekeeper thinking "this cover letter was so damn good I don't need to see the resume. My mind is made up. As long as the resume doesn't have glaring mistakes, missing dates, major flaws, I am inviting this person in for an interview."

If this is done well your resume is *almost* not needed. All your resume has to do is not tick the person off. You could send a page with your name and address at the top and have it blank underneath and you'd still get an interview.

Okay, I think you're almost ready.

The Perfect Resume

LET'S REVIEW SOME OF WHAT we've learned so far—and throw in a few more rules too.

Rules for the perfect resume:

- Use the fewest amount of words you can.

- Choose the proper word and make each one count. Words have impact!

- Use action words, not passive ones. (*Drove* sales to... *Pushed, Directed, Implemented, Initiated, Delivered, Launched.*)

- *Do not* write a resume in first person. It makes you come across as conceited. Only I, the omnipotent one, am allowed to do that. So, look for I, me, my, and get rid of them.

- *Do not* refer to yourself when writing in third person. It makes you come across as...just take my word for it—don't do it. Example: *Don't* say she designed a new switch...or he increased sales 25%. Eliminate the pronouns and simply say, "designed a new switch...or increased sales 25%."

- *Do not* put your religion on paper.

- *Do not* add unnecessary personal information. We don't want to know your wife's name, or your children's names, or your social security number. (Yes, I actually have had *several* people include that on the resume, along with their date of birth and address.)

- *Do not* put your hobbies on the resume. Even *if* you have a black belt in a martial art, or run marathons, or are an expert photographer. *I* don't care about it, and neither will the gatekeeper.

- *Do not* put the reason you were let go, or say that you were laid off. Leave that explanation for the interview.

- *Do* cite accomplishments over responsibilities. Yes. I *am* interested in seeing what you have accomplished in your jobs.

- *Do* include details on the dates of past employment, even if they show a gap. Yes, I *do* want to know about those.

- *Do* include education. Like it or not, education is a mandatory question from *all* companies. I suggest putting it at the top of the resume, not the bottom.

Conclusion

I will conclude with a few statements about this book. I offered strong opinions on what to do and, more specifically, what not to do.

Let's take a look:

No Objective—what I'm really saying is that an objective won't necessarily trash your resume, but it *might*.

No Summary—same thing with summaries. Having one on your resume won't automatically sentence it to the wastebasket—but it *could*.

Education—putting your education section in the wrong place is not the death knell I made it out to be—but it *can* hurt.

Having a personal section, or hobbies, or anything else—might not kill your chances—but they *could*, depending on who reviews your file.

Think about this for a moment.

None of the things I tell you to leave off your resume will hurt you because they *aren't* there, but they *might* hurt you if they *are* there. **Why risk it?**

Okay, let's wrap this up with a few quick mentions about impact words.

Impact Words

YOUR RESUME SHOULD BE FILLED with impact words. Words can be *very* powerful. Think of the emotions some of these simple statements generate:

"I *love* you."

"I *hate* you."

"You are *so* beautiful."

These are simple, but *strong* words, and they have power! They conjure up images, evoke emotions, and stir feelings—both positive and negative. That is why it is important for you to pay attention to the words you use on your resume.

What images do these words bring to mind?

- Spider, snake, scorpion
- Pit Bull, Doberman Pinscher, Rottweiler
- Kittens, puppies
- Facilitate, utilize

Each of those words evokes an image, but together they are much stronger; they reinforce each other. So when you think *spider, snake, and scorpion*, all in one thought, the feeling you get is probably one of danger, or at least apprehension.

The next grouping, *Pit Bull, Doberman, and Rottweiler,* may elicit a somewhat similar reaction, though probably not as primal. More of a warning.

And the third set—*kittens and puppies*—unless you're an animal hater, should generate a warm feeling, maybe even a smile.

But how about the final two words: *facilitate and utilize?* Anything? Kind of bland, aren't they? Yet they are two of the most common words found on resumes. Hunt them down and destroy them. Replace them with better words, like *use* and *ease*.

When you *use* words like *utilize* and *facilitate* on a resume, the focus of attention is on them. Replace them with simpler words that let the sentence flow. If you have stronger words on your resume, think about how you could rewrite the whole sentence to make it more powerful.

Back to Power Words

Resume words can be powerful. Not to the extent of the examples I used, but similar. Think of these words: *built, completed, discovered.* For some of you, *built* may conjure images of a toolshed you built, or a fence around your property, or new shelves in your bedroom closet. You may have *completed*, a project that you put off for months, or you finished paying off that car loan. The image could be something as simple as *discovering*, a new route home to avoid traffic, or a new way to cook your favorite meal.

One thing these words have in common is that they stir good feelings. When you see them on a resume, no matter who you are, you can't help but feel positive reinforcement. What nouns you use to follow those verbs will determine how the gatekeeper feels about them, and that is why it is so important to create a new resume for each position, tailored to the needs of the job description.

"Built a marketing team from scratch for new disk-drive product."

"Completed design of a new generator on time and under budget."

"Discovered new process for small-molecule drug formulation."

If the gatekeeper needs a new marketing team built, or a new generator designed, or a new drug formulated, you can bet your resume will get maximum attention.

There are hundreds of impact words to use on resumes, but the ones I've included here are among the most powerful. Look at them. What do you think when you see them?

Built

Completed

Created

Cut

Designed

Developed

Discovered

Eliminated

Established

Fixed

Generated

Improved

Increased

Invented

Launched

Led

Managed

Negotiated

Operated

Reduced

Saved

Sold

Solved

If you are applying for a position where cost-cutting measures could be valuable, consider some of these words from the list: *cut, eliminated, fixed, improved, negotiated, reduced, saved, solved.*

No matter what words you use on your resume, remember to *think* about them and what kind of message you're sending with them.

Words to Avoid

WE DIDN'T TALK MUCH ABOUT which words to avoid and why, so we'll cover that briefly in this chapter. This subject could take up a whole book, but you'll get the gist of it here. If you do a search on the internet for "words to avoid on your resume" or something to that effect, you'll find a fairly long list. I included some of the worst offenders.

Team player

Besides being a tired, old phrase, this falls into the "show, don't tell" rule. You can *tell* someone all day long that you're a team player, but if you don't know them, they're not going to believe you. You have to *show* that you're a team player through your actions. So instead of saying you're a "team player" *show* the gatekeeper something you *did* demonstrating that you are a team player.

- Developed and set up a program to train new engineers in the use of SolidWorks.

Results oriented

Instead of *telling* the gatekeeper you are "results oriented," *show* her.

- Designed and implemented a new quality system that improved yields by 13% in less than six months.

Resumes are rife with clichés and tired words that mean nothing. When gatekeepers read a resume, they gloss over those words as they try to find something interesting. Here is a partial list of words and phrases to avoid:

Bottom-line oriented

Cutting-edge

Detailed-oriented

Experienced

Goal-oriented

Highly skilled

Innovative

Motivated

Out-of-the-box thinker

Proven track record

Results-oriented

Self-starter

Strategic thinker

Team player

A good rule of thumb is this: unless your resume backs up the words you're using to describe yourself, don't use them.

And if your resume backs up those words, then you don't need to use them, because you'll be redundant.

In other words, *don't use them.*

A better rule to remember: *don't use adjectives to describe yourself.*

And an even better rule: *don't ever describe yourself. There's no reason to.*

You should *never* have to describe yourself on a resume. It's far better to let your accomplishments *show* who you are. State your name at the top then detail your work history and accomplishments. That's it.

Beliefs

To sum it up, here are my beliefs regarding resumes.

- I don't like to *utilize* words like *facilitate* when writing a resume. Big words often leave me confused, and I believe that people have a tendency to be redundant when using them.

- I believe objectives sections should be obliterated. They occupy valuable space and make you look bad.

- I believe that summaries sections are all tell and no show. I believe they're redundant and should be scratched.

- I believe that skills sections should be scrutinized before each use.

- I believe the entire resume should be perused, and then perused again, before hitting the send button.

- I believe personal sections should be kept personal— and not included on the resume.

- I believe education sections should show education only.

- I believe that two-dollar words should be reduced to fifty-cent ones.

- I believe the companies you worked for should be described.

- I believe dates should be accurate.

- I believe *lying* should be omitted and omissions should be revealed.

- I believe references should be purged.

- I believe publications and patents should be offered as attachments.

- I believe resumes should never go out alone; they should always be accompanied by a cover letter.

- I believe mistakes should be sought out, hunted down, surgically removed, and…banished.

And finally…

- I believe that resumes should be *perfect*.

One more thing

I firmly believe you should sign up for my newsletter so you can be alerted of new books and bonus material. You can go to my website: http://nomistakes.org

Or follow this link: http://eepurl.com/kS-IX

The website will continually be updated with new material and free stuff. In fact, you'll get a free *No Mistakes Resumes* checklist just for signing up.

---

1 Many people think to *peruse* means *to glance over* or *to skim*, when it means the opposite. *Peruse* means *to read thoroughly*.

2 Many people use "bold-faced" lie instead of "bald-faced," but the original saying was "bald-faced" or "barefaced" lie.

Did I leave something out? Do you still have questions? If there are other things you'd like to see covered, send me an email and let me know: jg@nomistakesresumes.com

If you enjoyed this book, keep an eye out for the next one in the series—*No Mistakes Interviews.*

Authors live and die by recommendations to friends, and reviews, so if you have a few minutes, would you consider leaving an honest review on Amazon, Apple, B&N, or Goodreads? It doesn't have to be a five-star review, and it doesn't have to be literary. Just say what you felt about the book. Did it help you? Teach you anything you didn't know before? I know leaving a review is a pain in the ass, but they really help authors.

And if you're interested in mystery/suspense books, check out my other novels. http://giacomogiammatteo.com

Last thing.

Remember I mentioned free things if you sign up for the newsletter. Sign up now and you'll get a free resume checklist that covers items mentioned in this book. What are you waiting for? Go get it.

http://nomistakes.org

About the Author

I know I'm supposed to have a professional head shot and be standing against a tree or in front of a fireplace with my arm resting on the mantel, but…that's not me. So here I am, with one of my favorite dogs of all time—Slick. (Please don't tell the other dogs I said that.)

As far as background, I've been a headhunter for 30 years, doing retained searches in the medical device/diagnostics & biotech/pharma industries. I have completed more than 500 searches, which translates into evaluating, editing, and writing thousands of resumes. I've also interviewed and done reference checks on more than 1,000 candidates. What does all that mean? It means I've seen a lot of crazy…stuff.

If I had let it get to me, I could have ended up in a small room with padded walls. I decided to write books instead. A couple of my books have hit "bestseller" status, (whatever the hell that means) but as long as people are enjoying them, I'm happy. You can check out my mystery/suspense books here: giacomog.com

Getting back to the bio—when I'm not headhunting, or writing, I help my wife take care of our animal sanctuary. At last count we had 45 animals—11 dogs, 1 horse, 6 cats, and 26 pigs.

Oh, and one crazy—and very large—wild boar named Dennis who takes walks with me every day and happens to also be my best buddy.

Now that you've read the book, check out the website. Look around, click some links, and, if you've got time, tell me what you think. Contact me at jg@nomistakes.org

CPSIA information can be obtained at www.ICGtesting.com
Printed in the USA
LVOW08s1350141013

356840LV00003B/94/P